ZENSCAPES
COLORING BOOK

Jessica Mazurkiewicz

Dover Publications, Inc.
Mineola, New York

The swirling, undulating images in this remarkable coloring book will invite you into a world of Zen, providing meditative thoughts and calming patterns. Enjoy selecting colors to express your connection to these pages as you perceive the vibrating quality of the lines—you'll find the relaxing nature of repetition and the suggestions of infinity quite soothing. Once you are satisfied with your work, you can remove the perforated, unbacked pages for easy display.

Bibliographical Note
Zenscapes Coloring Book is a new work, first published by
Dover Publications, Inc., in 2015.

International Standard Book Number
ISBN-13: 978-0-486-78054-2
ISBN-10: 0-486-78054-6

Manufactured in the United States by RR Donnelley
78054605   2015
www.doverpublications.com